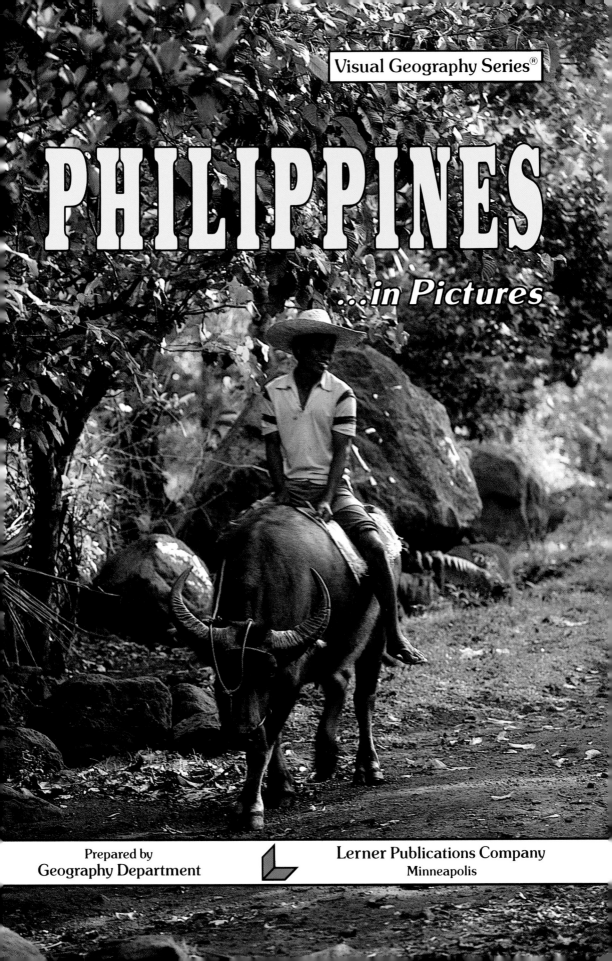

Visual Geography Series®

PHILIPPINES

...in Pictures

Prepared by
Geography Department

Lerner Publications Company
Minneapolis

Courtesy of Philippine Department of Tourism, Manila

A Filipino woman's skill at weaving captures the attention of her grandchild.

This is an all-new edition of the Visual Geography Series. Previous editions have been published by Sterling Publishing Company, New York City, and some of the original textual information has been retained. New photographs, maps, charts, captions, and updated information have been added. The text has been entirely reset in 10/12 Century Textbook.

LIBRARY OF CONGRESS CATALOGING-IN-PUBLICATION DATA

Philippines in pictures / prepared by Geography Department, Lerner Publications Company.

   p. cm. – (Visual geography series)
   Rev. ed. of: The Philippines in pictures / prepared by Leticia V. Ramos-Shahani.
   Includes index.
   Summary: Introduces the land, history, people, economy, and government of the more than seven thousand islands comprising the Philippines.
   ISBN 0-8225-1863-5
   1. Philippines. [1. Philippines.] I. Ramos-Shahani, Leticia V. Philippines in pictures. II. Lerner Publications Company. Geography Dept. III. Series: Visual geography series (Minneapolis, Minn.)
DS655.P624   1989
959.9-dc19
                    89–2296
                    CIP
                    AC

International Standard Book Number: 0-8225-1863-5
Library of Congress Catalog Card Number: 89-2296

VISUAL GEOGRAPHY SERIES®

Publisher
Harry Jonas Lerner
Associate Publisher
Nancy M. Campbell
Senior Editor
Mary M. Rodgers
Editors
Gretchen Bratvold
Dan Filbin
Photo Researcher
Karen A. Sirvaitis
Editorial/Photo Assistant
Marybeth Campbell
Consultant/Contributor
Maria Theresa Carl, Ph.D.
Sandra K. Davis
Designer
Jim Simondet
Cartographer
Carol F. Barrett
Indexer
Kristine S. Schubert
Sylvia Timian
Production Manager
Gary J. Hansen

Courtesy of Philippines Tourism Office

Rural Filipinos pitch in to move a house made of rattan and nipa palm.

Acknowledgements

Title page photo by Ken Meter.

Elevation contours adapted from *The Times Atlas of the World*, seventh comprehensive edition (New York: Times Books, 1985).

1   2   3   4   5   6   7   8   9   10   98   97   96   95   94   93   92   91   90   89

Courtesy of Agency for International Development

Wearing hats for protection from the sun, Filipino women plant rice—the country's most important food. The Philippines grows almost enough of this grain to meet the needs of its people, but when harvests are poor the nation must import rice. The national name "Philippines" shows the English language spelling of Philip, the sixteenth-century Spanish king after whom the islands were named. The name for the country's citizens, "Filipinos," more closely reflects the spelling of the monarch's Spanish name, Felipe.

Contents

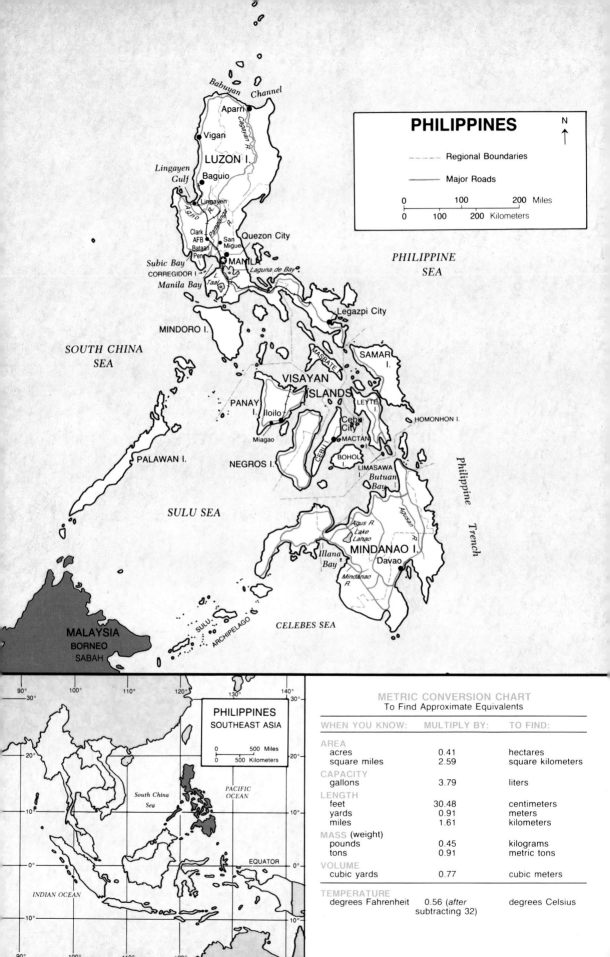

PHILIPPINES

N

- – – – Regional Boundaries
- ——— Major Roads

| 0 | 100 | 200 Miles |
| 0 | 100 | 200 Kilometers |

Babuyan Channel

Aparri

Cagayan R.

Vigan

LUZON I.

Lingayen Gulf

Baguio

Lingayen

Agno R.

Pampanga R.

Clark AFB

San Miguel

Bataan Pen.

Quezon City

Subic Bay

MANILA

CORREGIDOR I.

Laguna de Bay

Manila Bay

Taal

PHILIPPINE SEA

MINDORO I.

Legazpi City

SOUTH CHINA SEA

MASBATE

SAMAR I.

VISAYAN ISLANDS

PANAY I.

Iloilo

LEYTE

Miagao

Cebu City

CEBU

MACTAN

HOMONHON I.

NEGROS I.

BOHOL

LIMASAWA I.

Butuan Bay

Philippine Trench

SULU SEA

Agus R.

Lake Lanao

Agusan R.

Illana Bay

MINDANAO I.

Davao

Mindanao R.

SULU ARCHIPELAGO

CELEBES SEA

MALAYSIA

BORNEO

SABAH

PHILIPPINES
SOUTHEAST ASIA

| 0 | 500 Miles |
| 0 | 500 Kilometers |

90° 100° 110° 120° 130° 140°

30° 30°

20° 20°

South China Sea

PACIFIC OCEAN

10° 10°

0° 0° EQUATOR

INDIAN OCEAN

10° 10°

Throngs of people fill a street in Manila, the capital of the Philippines. In the twentieth century, the city's population increases at a faster rate than that of the rest of the nation. Religious and cultural traditions encourage Filipinos to value large families, and many members of rural communities have moved to the cities.

Photo by Ken Meter

Introduction

A nation made up of thousands of islands in the western Pacific Ocean, the Republic of the Philippines contains over 80 ethnic groups. Most Filipinos trace their roots to the Asian mainland or to early island kingdoms located west of the Philippines. Malays—who came from the territories of present-day Indonesia and Malaysia

during the last 12,000 years—are the largest group to have established communities on the islands. These Malays and other immigrants form the many ethnic roots of the modern Filipino population.

For centuries, the Philippines was a colony of other nations. Its relationships with its former rulers—Spain and later the United States—live on in the religions, languages, and culture of the Philippines. Christian missionaries arrived in the sixteenth century as part of a Spanish attempt to colonize the region. They brought the Spanish language as well as Christianity to the islands. The United States took over the archipelago (group of islands) in 1898 and introduced the English tongue. After the Philippines gained independence in 1946, Pilipino became the official language of the country.

Since 1946, the Filipinos have turned their attention to long-standing internal problems. High on this list of concerns is land distribution. For centuries, huge parcels of land belonged to a small group of landowners. Poorly paid workers farmed these acreages. Since independence, Philippine governments have introduced land reform programs in order to redistribute territory to the nation's landless tenant farmers. Wealthy landowners, however, have hampered the reform efforts.

In 1986—after years of slow economic growth and widespread government corruption—Filipino voters rejected the leadership of Ferdinand Marcos, who had been president since 1965. They elected Corazon Aquino to head the nation, and her administration has helped to boost the economy. Land redistribution has not been fully achieved, but Aquino continues to work for change through the Filipino legislature.

Aquino's government faces continued pressure from Communist rebels, from religious minorities, and from Filipinos who are still loyal to Marcos. Political stability and economic development are the primary goals of the Philippine government.

Crowds in Manila applaud a speaker at a victory celebration after the election of Corazon Aquino. She was elected president in February 1986.

Sandy bays are common throughout the more than 7,000 islands that make up the Philippines. This beach is in Antique, on the western side of Panay Island, which is located in the western Visayans.

Courtesy of Philippine Department of Tourism, Manila

1) The Land

The Philippine Islands lie at the western edge of the Pacific Ocean. To the north is the island of Taiwan. To the west, beyond the South China Sea, are Vietnam and China. The Philippines faces Malaysia and Indonesia across the Sulu and Celebes seas in the southwest. The portion of the Pacific Ocean on the eastern side of the archipelago is named the Philippine Sea.

Stretching across 1,100 miles of ocean, the Philippines contains over 7,000 islands. Only about 150 of them, however, are bigger than five square miles in area. The nation's total land area is almost 116,000 square miles, making it slightly larger than the state of Nevada.

Topography

The territory of the Philippines may be divided into three main areas, each of which is represented by a star on the national flag. Luzon (40,400 square miles), the

7

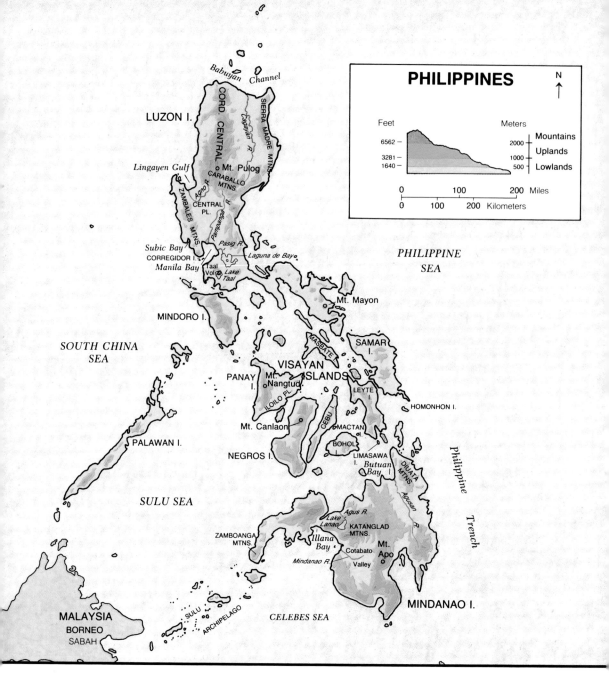

PHILIPPINES

Feet | Meters
6562 — | 2000 — Mountains
3281 — | 1000 — Uplands
1640 — | 500 — Lowlands

0   100   200 Miles
0   100   200 Kilometers

largest island in the archipelago, anchors the northern end of the island chain. Mindanao (36,500 square miles) ranks as the second biggest landmass and sits at the archipelago's southern tip. Between these two pieces of territory lie islands that are known collectively as the Visayans.

Not all Philippine territories fit into these three main categories. For example, west of the main body of the archipelago lies Palawan Island, a narrow strip of mountainous territory. Mindoro, an oval-shaped island between Palawan and Luzon, has a central mountain range and a wide coastal plain on its eastern side. A number of smaller islands also fall outside of the country's three principal geographical divisions.

Volcanic action and movements of the earth's crust formed the Philippine Islands, most of which are mountainous. About 20 of the country's peaks are active volcanoes. Long coastlines, which offer harbors for shipping and access to fishing waters, are also a main feature of the Philippines.

LUZON

Several mountain ranges run through Luzon—the archipelago's largest island. The Sierra Madre extend for over 200 miles along Luzon's northeastern coast and range from 3,500 to 5,000 feet in height. The rolling plain of the Cagayan Valley lies between the Sierra Madre and the Cordillera Central—the main range on Luzon. The Cordillera's peaks reach a height of 9,606 feet at Mount Pulog. In central Luzon, this range meets the Caraballo Mountains, which have an elevation of 2,000 to 5,000 feet. The flat central plain

of the island extends westward from the Caraballos to the Zambales Mountains, a small chain that pushes south into the Bataan Peninsula.

Manila Bay, the site of the nation's capital city of Manila, is a 770-square-mile inlet of the South China Sea on Luzon's west coast. Corregidor Island guards the inlet's mouth. Located less than 100 miles south of Manila, the Taal Volcano has erupted nine times since the eighteenth century. The most recent upheaval occurred in 1968. Mount Mayon, another active volcano, stands at a height of 8,284 feet in southeastern Luzon. This volcano's cone is often hidden in water vapor from the crater.

THE VISAYAN ISLANDS

Composed of more than 6,000 pieces of territory, the Visayan Islands have seven principal landmasses. The easternmost of

Photo by Ken Meter

Mount Mayon, an 8,000-foot peak in southern Luzon, emits a plume of vapor from its crater. Many active volcanos dot the Philippines.

A river cuts through rich but rocky volcanic soil in southern Luzon. Palm trees in the background indicate the fury of a recent storm.

Photo by Ken Meter

the seven is Samar, which has low, rugged mountains covered with dense rain-forests. Samar receives heavy rainfall from annual typhoons (hurricane-like storms that form in the western Pacific). Leyte, lying west of Samar, has mountains that run through the center of the island and rise to over 4,000 feet. With coastal areas that are wider than those of Samar, Leyte supports fields of coconuts, corn, rice, and abacas (from which rope is made).

Centrally located in the Visayan group, Cebu Island is one of the most populous of the Philippine Islands. A long, narrow landmass with central mountains extending its entire length, Cebu's highest point is 3,324 feet above sea level. Cebu has very limited level land, which restricts agricultural activities on the island. South of Cebu, the round island of Bohol has a large lowland area and mountains that reach an elevation of 2,600 feet. Bohol's smooth

The Chocolate Hills—which are made of limestone, shale, and sandstone—stretch for miles along the island of Bohol. The sparse grass changes from green to brown in the dry summer, causing the mounds to resemble large chocolate drops.

Independent Picture Service

Courtesy of Philippines Tourism Office

Climbers work their way up Mount Apo, the highest peak in the Philippines. Located near Davao on the island of Mindanao, the mountain is the home of the *haribon*, or Philippine eagle. Reaching the summit requires four or five days of climbing.

coastline offers few good places for ships to anchor.

Lying west of Cebu is Negros Island, with a largely mountainous topography except for coastal plains to the north. The island's highest peak is Mount Canlaon, an active volcano that rises 8,070 feet above sea level. Volcanic lava, which has spread over the island during centuries of eruptions, has enriched the soil of Negros.

Panay lies next to Negros and is the westernmost of the Visayan group. The island's mountains run parallel to the western coast, and Mount Nangtud (6,724 feet) is the tallest. A feature of central Panay is a large lowland area, which is matched in the southeast by the Iloilo Plain. Masbate is the northernmost major island of the Visayan group. Low mountains cover Masbate, which is the Philippines' main gold-producing region.

MINDANAO

The second largest island of the Philippines, Mindanao is shaped like an irregular triangle. Its coastline has many bays and inlets. Just off the eastern coast of this island is the Philippine Trench—a huge depression in the Philippine Sea. At its deepest point, the trench descends 34,578 feet below the water's surface.

On the eastern coast of Mindanao, the Diuata Mountains rise to over 6,000 feet. The Agusan River Valley extends for about 50 miles west of these mountains. In central Mindanao, the Katanglad Mountains reach almost 9,000 feet above sea level. Located near the city of Davao, Mount Apo—an active volcano that rises to 9,690 feet—is the highest mountain in the Philippines. The Cotabato Valley reaches westward from the center of the island, and the Zamboanga Mountains stand on a peninsula that juts into the Sulu Sea.

Rivers and Lakes

The Philippine Islands have many rivers, most of which are short and swift. The heavy rainfall that accompanies the region's monsoons (seasonal winds) often floods the rivers. Luzon and Mindanao contain the longest and most important rivers.

Much of the Cagayan River in northern Luzon is navigable. As it flows northward along its 220-mile course, this river irrigates the 50-mile-wide valley between the Sierra Madre and the Cordillera Central. After passing the coastal city of Aparri, the Cagayan empties into the Babuyan Channel.

The Pampanga River, another major waterway on Luzon, begins in the Caraballo Mountains and flows south for 120 miles into Manila Bay. The central plain, which receives the Pampanga's waters, is one of the most fertile areas in the Philippines. Beginning in the Cordillera Central, the Agno River turns west and irrigates

11

another wide plain before emptying into Lingayen Bay.

In eastern Mindanao, the Agusan River extends 240 miles as it travels north to Butuan Bay. The fertile valley that the Agusan creates is 50 miles wide and supports large rice and corn crops. The Mindanao River begins in the central part of the island and flows south and west for over 100 miles before reaching Illana Bay. Small boats navigate much of the Mindanao River, and the waterway's tributaries make the surrounding territory a highly productive agricultural area.

Although it has many small lakes, the Philippines contains only three lakes of considerable size. Laguna de Bay lies in central Luzon near Manila. The largest lake in the Philippines, it covers 344 square miles. The 14-mile-long Pasig River carries overflow from the lake through the capital city into Manila Bay.

Forty miles south of Manila is the 94-square-mile Lake Taal. Situated within the collapsed cone of a dead volcano, Lake Taal contains a small, active volcano that forms an island in its center.

Mindanao's Lake Lanao sits on a plateau north of the Katanglad Mountains and occupies an area of 131 square miles. The Agus River provides Lake Lanao's outlet to the sea.

Climate

The Philippines has a rainy season and a dry season. The weather on the islands changes depending on the direction of the monsoons. When the southwest monsoon blows from May to November, the Philippine Islands receive plenty of rain from the moisture-laden winds. In lowland areas, the average rainfall is over 80 inches during this season, while in the mountains, up

Courtesy of Philippine Department of Tourism, Manila

The waters of Lake Taal—which is located south of Manila—fill the collapsed cone of Taal Volcano, the lowest volcano in the world. A newer crater rises out of the lake and it, in turn, contains its own lake.

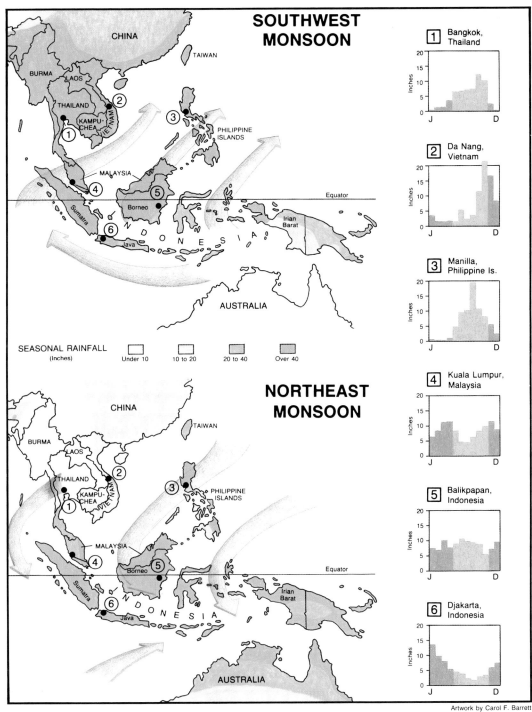

SOUTHWEST MONSOON

1 Bangkok, Thailand

2 Da Nang, Vietnam

3 Manilla, Philippine Is.

4 Kuala Lumpur, Malaysia

5 Balikpapan, Indonesia

6 Djakarta, Indonesia

SEASONAL RAINFALL (Inches)
Under 10 | 10 to 20 | 20 to 40 | Over 40

NORTHEAST MONSOON

Artwork by Carol F. Barrett

These maps show the seasonal shift of winds, called monsoons, over Southeast Asia and the rainfall levels for six cities in the region. From May to October, the winds blow from the southwest. From November to April, they come from the northeast. Because the monsoons in Southeast Asia travel over the ocean, they bring rain to coastal and island areas. The southwest monsoon carries rain to Southeast Asia and to islands north of the equator. These areas are dry during the northeast monsoon period. Islands south of the equator receive moisture from the northeast monsoon but are relatively dry during the southwest monsoon period. Both monsoons bring rain to islands on the equator. Manila receives most of its rainfall during the southwest monsoon. The rain-bearing winds sweep in from the sea and rise over the highlands to the east and north of the city. During the northeast monsoon, however, these same highlands divert the windflow, and little rain falls on the city. (Data taken from *World-Climates* by Willy Rudloff, Stuttgart, 1981.)

Filipino farmers place rice plants in flooded fields called paddies. Rice is cultivated throughout lowland areas of the Philippines, but the elevated fertile plains of central Luzon produce the highest yields of rice.

Courtesy of Agency for International Development

to 150 inches are common. Although many fields often flood, farmers who grow rice use the flood water to irrigate their crops. Temperatures hover around 80° F during the rainy season.

In December the direction of the wind changes, and the northeast monsoon starts to blow. Lasting until April, the northeast monsoon causes several months of cooler weather for much of the nation. Manila averages 75° F in January, and in some areas the temperature occasionally falls below 70° F. By April, however, Manila's temperatures are back in the low eighties,

and highs of over 100° F are often recorded in other areas of the country.

From June until October, the Philippines also experiences a typhoon season. Typhoons are large, slow-moving storms that bring heavy rains. Winds that reach speeds of 150 miles per hour accompany the storms. A dozen or more typhoons sweep the Philippines each year. Five or six of them hit the islands with destructive force, ruining homes and sometimes killing people and livestock. Typhoons most often affect northern Luzon and the eastern Visayan Islands.

Flora and Fauna

Rain-forests cover the slopes of many Philippine mountains and some lowland areas. Sunlight, warmth, rain, and fertile soil cause some trees in these forests to grow 150 feet tall, creating a leafy canopy. Beneath the shade of the treetops thrive vines, epiphytes (air plants), and climbing palms. Pine forests are common at higher elevations. Stands of Philippine mahogany, banyan (part of the mulberry family), and molave (a tree with hard, yellow wood) can also be found on the archipelago.

Courtesy of Philippines Tourism Office

A waterfall cascades down rocks in a rain-forest located a short distance from Manila. Among the vegetation growing beneath this 100-foot leafy canopy are air plants, which absorb moisture and air through their leaves.

Courtesy of Jodi M. Bantley

A man at the top of a coconut palm taps the tree for its juice. Filipinos use the liquid to make a drink called *tuba,* which is drunk fresh or is made into an alcoholic beverage known as *lambanog.*

Courtesy of Philippines Tourism Office

A Filipino woman sells papayas, bananas, and melons at an open-air market.

More than 800 species of orchids thrive in the rain-forests of the Philippines. The sweetly scented orchid *(above)* is the country's national flower. Filipinos welcome distinguished visitors by giving them leis (necklaces made of flowers) and orchid corsages.

The Philippine eagle—which is also called the monkey-eating eagle—is the national emblem of the Philippines. At one time, the species was in danger of extinction. In the last two decades, however, a breeding program has increased the number of these birds.

Cogon grows on many of the plateaus throughout the islands. The grass forms a dense turf and has roots that are highly resistant to fire. Bamboo plants sprout thickly along many of the islands' coasts and rivers. The Philippines' national flower is the sampaguita orchid, one of more than 9,000 flowering plants in the country.

The islands host a variety of animals. Small, wild buffalo known as tamarau roam the mountains of Mindoro. Tarsiers —mammals that live mostly in trees and have owl-like eyes—probably came to the territory centuries ago from India. Mouse deer—a species of small, red deer—live on Palawan Island. Water buffalo, called carabao, are the main domestic animals in the Philippines. The forests of the country contain many varieties of monkeys.

Once found throughout the region, crocodiles now inhabit only remote regions of Palawan and Mindanao. Pythons, water

The tarsier, the world's smallest monkey, inhabits the rainforests of Bohol, Leyte, and Mindanao. The tarsier's large eyes enable it to see well at night, when the animal is active.

snakes, and other varieties of snakes are common throughout the islands. Geckos (small lizards) eat insects and are sometimes kept as pets by young Filipinos. Monitor lizards find suitable habitats throughout the countryside. The Philippine eagle—the world's largest eagle species —preys upon geckos and monitor lizards. Parrots, found predominantly on Palawan, have brightly colored feathers and are often exported to other countries as pets.

Cities

The cities of the Philippines contained 41 percent of the nation's population in 1989. Manila is the capital and largest city of the Philippines. It is also the commercial hub, principal port city, and financial center of the country.

Located in southwestern Luzon, Manila grew from over a dozen small cities and towns that were clustered along Manila Bay. In the late 1980s, the city contained 1.6 million people, while the population in the wider metropolitan area was over 8 million.

Courtesy of Jodi M. Bantley

A carabao, or water buffalo, pulls a plow through a corn field. The Philippines devotes almost as much land to corn production as it does to rice cultivation.

Courtesy of Jodi M. Bantley

As increasing numbers of farm families move into Filipino cities, slum settlements expand to accommodate the newcomers.

Filipinos board a double-decker bus in Manila. A number of bus companies carry passengers throughout the capital and to other areas of the island of Luzon.

The suburb of Makati provides a view of the main part of Manila. In the 1960s, the Makati area was marshland. By the late 1980s, glass and concrete buildings housed offices of multinational companies, banks, the stock exchange, hotels, retail stores, and art galleries.

The Pasig River divides Manila in half. South of the river lies Intramuros, an old walled city that was built by the Spanish. Farther south is Rizal Park (also known as Luneta)—a large, open space that serves as a central meeting place for the city's inhabitants. Among the neighborhoods north of the river is Tondo, a community with overcrowded, makeshift housing. Manila also is the site of Malacañang Palace, the president's official residence.

Bordering Manila on the northeast is Quezon City, the nation's capital from 1948 until 1976. Although Manila is the capital, many government offices continue to operate from Quezon City. The central campus of the University of the Philippines is also located in Quezon City.

Cebu City, on the eastern coast of the island of Cebu, has a thriving harbor. Most of the imports and exports of the Visayan Islands arrive and depart through this port. With a population of more than 500,000 people, Cebu is one of the Philippines' largest cities. Among the first Spanish settlements in the archipelago, Cebu City contains sixteenth-century Fort San Pedro, as well as many Spanish-style churches. Several universities are located within the city, including Southwestern University, which was founded in 1950.

Another major port city is Iloilo on southeastern Panay Island. Because pirates often raided the settlement during the 1700s and 1800s, residents built many stone watchtowers and defensive forts. In the late 1980s, Iloilo was a major agricultural trading center with over 250,000 inhabitants. The city is also the commercial center for the island's rapidly growing textile industry.

Davao lies on the southeastern coast of Mindanao Island and is one of the fastest-growing cities in the nation. With over 800,000 people, Davao draws many immigrants from other Philippine islands. These Filipinos seek jobs as farm workers in the surrounding region. Coconuts are exported through Davao's port to world markets.

Courtesy of Jodi M. Bantley

Open-air markets in Philippine cities and towns offer a variety of handicrafts and colorful sights to visitors, as well as Filipinos.

Courtesy of Jodi M. Bantley

A Spanish-style Catholic church in central Luzon reflects the influence of Spain on the culture and religion of the Philippines.

For several centuries, the efforts of Igorots (mountain ethnic groups) have produced terraces that make it possible for these farmers to grow rice in the highlands.

2) History and Government

In Luzon's Cagayan Valley, archaeologists have discovered stone tools and remains of campsites that belonged to the ancient inhabitants of the Philippine Islands. These materials date from 250,000 years ago, when the region was still connected to Asia by land.

Waves of ethnic groups from different parts of Asia came to the Philippines by an overland route. About 25,000 years ago the Aeta people—hunters who used bows and arrows—arrived in the territory.

Other people migrated from the neighboring island of Borneo about 12,000 years later. These newcomers planted and harvested crops in addition to hunting for their food. Roughly 12,000 years ago, sheets of ice that covered large areas of the earth's surface melted. The water submerged the land routes that connected the Philippines to other parts of Asia. From this time on, the Philippines were islands.

Between 1500 and 500 B.C., Malays and people from what are now China and Vietnam came to the region in oceangoing canoes. As these newcomers settled along the coasts, the inhabitants who already lived in the archipelago moved to the interior of the islands. The new arrivals used tools and weapons of polished stone and grouped their dwellings in villages. The newer Malay immigrants introduced carabao as work animals. These Malays and their descendants also cultivated rice on terraces cut into the mountainsides of northern Luzon. Malay people continued to come to the islands in large numbers for many centuries.

Contact with Ancient Kingdoms

The location of the Philippines between the Indian and the Pacific oceans made it a convenient stopping place for sea traders. Many merchants came from the kingdom of Sri Vijaya, which was situated southwest of the Philippines on the island of Sumatra. By the A.D. 600s, Sri Vijaya was a major Pacific trading power.

Sri Vijaya controlled many of the sea routes throughout Southeast Asian waters, including those through the Philippines. Sri Vijayan control of trade in the Philippines and in the rest of Southeast Asia

Courtesy of Philippine Department of Tourism, Manila

Members of the Ifugao people on Luzon dance to the accompaniment of musicians. Handed down from generation to generation, village celebrations recall the ancient way of life of the Ifugao.

Artwork by Laura Westlund

An Indian philosopher named Gautama Buddha founded Buddhism as a way of overcoming human suffering and finding wisdom. Sri Vijayan traders from Indonesia first brought Buddhism to the Philippine Islands in the seventh century A.D.

lasted for about 500 years. Besides naming the Visayan Islands after themselves, the Sri Vijayans also influenced the religion of the archipelago. They introduced Filipinos to Buddhism—a faith inspired by Gautama Buddha in India during the sixth century B.C.

The Majapahit kingdom, which followed the Hindu religion, arose on the island of Java in the late 1200s. Soon Majapahit princes replaced the Sri Vijayans as controllers of the sea-lanes in the Philippines. Although the Majapahit leaders did not deliberately try to introduce Hinduism

Photo by Denver Art Museum

Siva is one of the major figures in Hinduism, a religion that began in India and predates Buddhism. When the Majapahit kingdom on the island of Java took control of southeast Asian sea-lanes in the thirteenth century, Majapahit sailors introduced Hinduism to the Philippines.

Muslims (followers of the Islamic religion) in a small village on Mindanao pray in their neighborhood mosque (house of prayer) each Friday. Arab and Malay Muslims brought Islam to the Philippines during the fourteenth century and were especially successful in spreading their religion in the southern islands.

into the regions they controlled, many elements of their Hindu culture came to the islands. For example, the Filipino *barong*—a distinctive shirt—is an adaptation of a garment worn by Hindus from southern India. Filipinos also adopted many words from Sanskrit, the language of Hinduism.

ARAB AND CHINESE TRADERS

During the eras of Sri Vijayan and Majapahit influence in the Philippines, Arab and Chinese traders also came to the islands. By the fourteenth century, Arab scholars had arrived in the southern part of the archipelago. They had success in spreading Islam—a religion founded in the seventh century A.D. in Arabia. By the middle of the fifteenth century, many people on the southern islands, especially Mindanao, had become Muslims (followers of Islam). Muslim traders from India, Malacca, and Borneo also came to the Philippines and helped to spread Islam.

Meanwhile, Chinese merchants approached the Philippines from the north. Landing most often on Luzon, these traders exchanged silk and porcelain for Philippine timber and gold. During the Chinese Ming era (1368–1644), the merchants established settlements on Luzon. The port of Lingayen, for example, took its name from a powerful Chinese trader called Lin Gaiyen.

Patterned after a Chinese architectural style, a temple in Cebu City serves the religious needs of many descendants of the Chinese traders who settled in this part of the Philippines. Chinese immigrants became politically as well as commercially powerful in the Philippines during the fifteenth century.

At the beginning of the fifteenth century, Chinese influence was so strong that Chinese leaders governed several of the northern islands. The Chinese clashed with Muslims from the south, however, and eventually lost many of their settlements on the islands. By the beginning of the 1500s, Muslims had extended their influence throughout much of Luzon.

Spanish Explorers

Beginning in the 1500s, European explorers searched for a short route to Asia's rich spice markets. In 1512 Ferdinand Magellan, a Portuguese-born navigator who sailed under the flag of Spain, traveled through Southeast Asian waters. His voyage took him to what are now Malaysia and Indonesia. A second expedition brought Magellan and his crew to Homonhon, a small island south of Leyte, in 1521. Traveling on to nearby Limasawa and Cebu, Magellan met friendly residents of these islands. The local people welcomed the Europeans and at first agreed to adopt the Christian religion.

Not everyone Magellan met, however, was friendly. Lapu-Lapu, ruler of the island of Mactan, refused to accept European ways or to be ruled by the advancing explorers. Magellan set out to conquer Lapu-Lapu and his followers, but Lapu-Lapu's warriors easily defeated the Europeans. Magellan was killed in the fighting on April 27, 1521. Survivors of the battle left the islands and continued their westward voyage around the world.

Despite this early defeat, the Spanish continued to explore the Pacific. Ruy Lopez de Villalobos landed on Mindanao in February 1545 and named the islands the Felipinas, after his Spanish patron, Prince Phillip (later King Phillip II).

Villalobos wanted to strengthen the Spanish claim to the islands by establishing permanent settlements in the archipelago. Lack of provisions and hostility from the local inhabitants hindered his plans. Nevertheless, the Spanish established their first colony at San Miguel, later known as the city of Cebu, on Cebu Island. Developed in 1565 by Miguel Lopez de Legazpi, the Spanish settlement housed 400 soldiers and several missionaries.

EARLY SPANISH RULE

Although the inhabitants strongly resented European control, Legazpi and his troops slowly brought the islanders under Spanish power. Occasionally more soldiers and missionaries arrived from Spain to reinforce Legazpi's efforts.

Many of the inhabitants of the archipelago became Christians at the urging of the missionaries. The Muslims (whom the Spanish called "Moros"), were the most difficult group for the soldiers to overcome and for the missionaries to convert. Large numbers of Moros in Mindanao successfully resisted the Spanish.

In 1571 Legazpi and his forces occupied Manila. The small population of Moros on Luzon fought the Spanish troops but eventually lost. Igorots—members of ethnic groups from the hills and mountains on Luzon—also resisted Spanish expansion and were difficult for the Europeans to conquer.

After defeating most of the resistant islanders, the colonizers made the region useful to their expanding empire. They established Manila as the central port for ships that carried silver from South America across the Pacific. Traders from China exchanged porcelain, silk, and textiles for Spanish gold at Manila's port. These early colonizers did little to develop the Philippine economy beyond introducing maize (corn) and improving the irrigation system in a few of the region's rice fields.

Photo by Bettmann Archive

Ferdinand Magellan and his crew landed in Philippine territory in 1521. After initial success, the Europeans met stiff resistance to their efforts to rule the Filipino population.

Independent Picture Service

This stamp commemorates Lapu-Lapu, who halted Magellan and his troops in 1521.

Spanish Occupation

The Spanish ruled the Philippines by expanding the system of organization that the people of the islands already used. The basic unit of government was the village, or barangay. Each village had a *datu* (ruler) who was chosen by informal agreement among the local residents. Roman Catholic priests lived in the barangays as missionaries and as representatives of the colonial administration. In these roles, they were able to strongly influence the selection of the datu.

The indirect rule of the Philippines by the Spanish missionaries was not successful in every region of the country. Diego Silang, a Filipino leader from northern Luzon, rebelled against the Spanish in 1762 and set up his own government in Vigan. The Moros on the southern islands raided Spanish military outposts and achieved independence in their own territories.

In the late eighteenth century, the Spanish used force to regain control over many of the rebellious groups in the country. The Europeans also introduced agricultural reforms. Administrators encouraged Filipino farmers to grow export crops such as abaca (from which rope is made), tea, and tobacco. The colonial government established a monopoly on the sale of tobacco that brought great wealth to Spanish officials.

In the early 1800s, the Spanish opened the Philippines to trade with merchants from Great Britain, the United States, France, and other nations. Sugarcane, abaca, and tobacco became major exports and helped to develop the Philippine economy.

Early Revolts

Although the colony's economy grew, most Filipinos did not benefit from increased trade. Missionaries, Spanish officials, and a few wealthy Filipinos owned most of the land and controlled commerce. The majority of Filipinos worked as tenant farmers and paid high rents to local landowners for the use of the land.

After gaining control of much of the Philippines in the sixteenth century, the Spanish built stone forts and watchtowers to protect their new colony. The ruins of this Spanish outpost are on the coast of Bohol.

José Rizal, a doctor and writer, led the first organized independence movement in the Philippines. Rizal's novels expressed the hope of many Filipinos for a nation free of foreign control. He was executed for his beliefs by the Spanish government in 1896.

The dissatisfaction of the Philippine population deepened, and several communities rebelled. The Ilocanos, an ethnic group from Luzon, revolted in 1807 when government officials took control of the region's wine-making industry. In 1841 many Filipinos joined their fellow islander Apolonario de la Cruz in an armed revolt on Luzon against Spanish oppression. Throughout the nineteenth century, many groups of Filipinos pressured Spanish leaders for economic reform and more political freedom. Lacking education or an official voice in colonial affairs, these Filipinos made little progress in improving conditions.

JOSE RIZAL

Among the small group of Filipinos who had studied at universities either in Manila or in Europe was José Rizal. By the end of the 1800s, he had become the most famous supporter of the cause of Philippine independence. A doctor and writer, Rizal established the Filipino League in 1891. His organization was dedicated to ending abuses of Spanish power, such as forcing laborers to work on plantations. The league's goal was to establish a self-governing Philippine nation.

Spanish officials exiled Rizal to northwestern Mindanao soon after he started his organization. When Rizal became a popular symbol of Filipino resistance, the Spanish executed him. Without Rizal's leadership, the Filipino League dissolved.

Revolution and War

In 1892 Andres Bonifacio founded the Katipunan (a word from the language of the Tagalog ethnic group that means "union"). This secret organization dedicated itself to overthrowing the Spanish colonizers through armed force. In 1896, 30,000 members of the Katipunan launched attacks against the Spanish.

Only one rebel leader, Emilio Aguinaldo, led his troops successfully against the Spanish, and he replaced Bonifacio as the Katipunan leader in 1897. Although the Spanish recaptured most of their territory, they failed to overcome Aguinaldo and his army. At the end of 1897, Aguinaldo signed the Biacna-Bato Pact with the colonizers. In the treaty, the Spanish promised self-rule for the Filipinos within three years if Aguinaldo would go into exile. In December 1897 the rebel leader sailed for Hong Kong.

Photo by Bettmann Archive

In 1897 Emilio Aguinaldo became the political and military leader of the Katipunan, an organization dedicated to Philippine self-rule. Aguinaldo pressed for independence first from Spain and later from the United States.

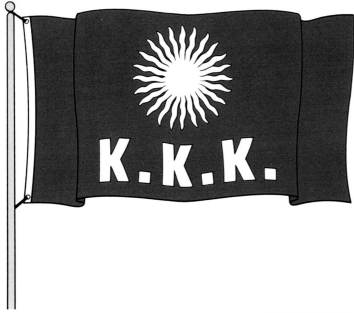

Artwork by Laura Westlund

The Katipunan flag contains a symbol of the sun, which represents independence. The three *K's* stand for the first three words of the movement's full name—Kataastaasan Kagalanggalang Katipunan.

Meanwhile, other parts of Spain's empire were rebelling. When the Caribbean island of Cuba declared independence from Spain, the United States supported the action. As a result, the United States and Spain confronted each other in the Spanish-American War in early 1898.

Among the colonial prizes at stake in the war was the Philippines. Commodore George Dewey brought the U.S. navy from Hong Kong into Manila Bay in April 1898, and by May 1 he had defeated the Spanish naval force. Aguinaldo returned from Hong Kong and led his Katipunan soldiers in the fight against the Spanish. In return for Katipunan assistance, the U.S. government promised independence for the Philippines.

Combined U.S. and Katipunan forces defeated the Spanish in August 1898. Later that year, the Treaty of Paris officially concluded the war between the United States and Spain. Under the treaty, the United States gained control of the Philippines, Guam, and Puerto Rico and in return gave Spain $20 million.

To many islanders, U.S. occupation was not an improvement over Spanish rule. Aguinaldo and many of the Filipino people resisted the U.S. presence. Rejecting any form of colonial control, Aguinaldo proclaimed national independence in 1899. Until his capture in 1901, he led armed resistance against U.S. forces. Remnants of his army continued to fight for another year without their leader.

U.S. Rule

In the early twentieth century, President William McKinley said that the United States did not intend to possess the Philippine Islands permanently. The United States accepted the idea of eventual independence for the Filipino people after a period of preparation for self-rule. As a result, education became a major focus for the U.S. administration of the islands.

Courtesy of U.S. Navy

In 1898 Commodore George Dewey brought ships of the United States Navy to Manila Bay after the start of the Spanish-American War. Within a few days, these naval forces controlled the entire bay area.

Courtesy of Library of Congress

U.S. president William McKinley *(above)* helped lay the foundation for eventual Philippine independence by appointing William Howard Taft as head of the Philippine Commission. Taft proposed a plan to establish the "Philippines for the Filipinos."

Photo by UPI/Bettmann Newsphotos

Manuel Luis Quezon y Molina pushed leaders in the United States to grant independence to the Philippines at an early date. Quezon became the first president of the country in 1935, when it was still a commonwealth nation under U.S. control.

Over 600 teachers from the United States came to the Philippines to help establish schools. Hundreds of U.S. citizens financially supported the University of the Philippines when it opened in Manila in 1908.

From the beginning of the period of U.S. control, Filipinos participated in governing the territory, although not fully enough for those who eagerly awaited national independence. Manuel Luis Quezon y Molina, Sergio Osmeña, and Manuel Roxas y Acuña were Filipino leaders who pushed U.S. officials for more self-rule in the Philippines.

As a result of Philippine concerns, the U.S. Congress passed the Tydings-McDuffie Act in 1934. The act provided for a Philippine constitution and for the election of a legislature and a president by the Philippine people. The Philippines would become a commonwealth nation—that is, it would govern itself internally, but the United States would retain control of foreign affairs and defense for a period of ten years. The Philippine people ratified the constitution in May 1935, and in November Quezon was elected president.

WORLD WAR II

On December 10, 1941, three days after World War II began in the Pacific, Japanese troops invaded the Philippines. Philippine and U.S. forces fought against the Japanese for several months, but the invaders pushed them into the Bataan Peninsula and onto Corregidor Island. On May 6, 1942, the Commonwealth of the Philippines surrendered, and the Japanese occupied the country. Quezon and other government leaders fled to Washington, D.C., to establish a government-in-exile.

The Japanese took most of the nation's rice to feed their soldiers throughout the Pacific, and many people in the Philippines starved. Most Filipinos refused to cooperate with harsh Japanese rule, and many actively resisted the enemy through guerrilla warfare.

SOVIET UNION

MONGOLIA

MANCHURIA

CHINA

KOREA

SAKHALIN ISLAND

ALEUTIAN IS.

KURIL ISLANDS

JAPAN

North Pacific Ocean

RYUKYU ISLANDS

BONIN ISLANDS

BURMA

THAILAND

TAIWAN

Okinawa

VOLCANO ISLANDS

Area of Japanese Control in 1942

PHILIPPINES

MARIANA ISLANDS

Wake

FRENCH INDOCHINA

Guam

MARSHALL ISLANDS

MALAYA

CAROLINE ISLANDS

SUMATRA

BORNEO

JAVA

NEW GUINEA

GILBERT ISLANDS

SOLOMON ISLANDS

N

AUSTRALIA

South Pacific Ocean

Artwork by Laura Westlund

In December 1941, when the Asian phase of World War II began, the Japanese struck quickly at many targets throughout Asia and the Pacific. By 1942 Japan controlled a vast area *(above)* that included the Philippines. In mid-1942, the Japanese took possession of the Philippines *(right)* after the many U.S. and Filipino troops had surrendered and other U.S. forces had withdrawn from the islands.

Photo by UPI/Bettmann Newsphotos

31

During the Japanese attack on the Philippines, the bombing of Manila destroyed many homes, roads, and buildings.

U.S. armed forces led by General Douglas MacArthur landed on Leyte Island on October 20, 1944. The battle to reclaim the islands from the Japanese lasted almost a year.

General Douglas MacArthur and his U.S. troops returned to the Philippines in October 1944. To aid the U.S. forces, Filipino guerrillas searched out the enemy and joined the United States in retaking the major islands from the Japanese. World War II came to an end when the Japanese surrendered on September 2, 1945.

Philippine Independence

Quezon died while leading the Philippine government-in-exile in the United States. Sergio Osmeña, his vice president, succeeded him and brought the government back to Manila in 1945. Manuel Roxas y Acuña won the presidential election held in April 1946. As chief executive, he began to rebuild the nation after the destruction of the war.

In accordance with the Tydings-McDuffie Act, the United States withdrew its authority over the Philippines. On July 4, 1946, the Republic of the Philippines achieved full independence. The U.S. government supported the new nation with economic assistance. In return, the Philippine government allowed the United States to keep military bases on the islands.

Along with the difficulties of rebuilding the nation after the war, the Filipino government also faced a challenge from Communist rebels. Called the People's Liberation Army (or Huks, a Tagalog abbreviation), the revolutionaries operated in central Luzon. The Huks wanted farmers' and workers' groups to have authority over land and industry. They believed Communist principles of shared landownership and equal distribution of income should guide these organizations.

In the early 1950s, Huk guerrillas attacked government forces. The rebels

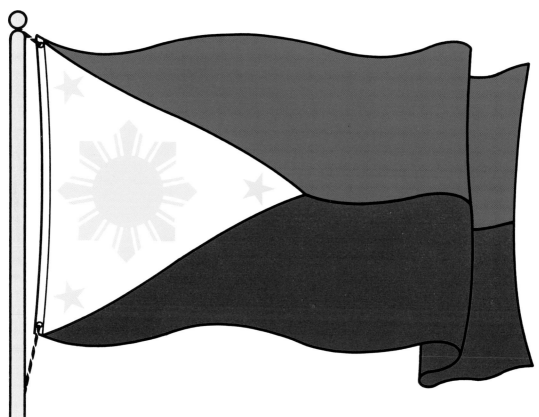

Artwork by Laura Westlund

The Philippine flag came into use during the independence movement in 1898. The white triangle signifies the Filipino struggle against colonial Spain. The stars represent the nation's three main regions — Luzon, the Visayans, and Mindanao. The sun with its eight rays symbolizes the eight provinces that first stood against Spanish occupation. The blue and red portions stand for generosity and courage, respectively.

gained support from many local people who were suffering from difficult postwar economic conditions. Ramón Magsaysay, the secretary of defense, led the Philippine army against the Huks. After his election as president in 1953, he effectively halted the Huk rebellion.

Challenges to the New Republic

Besides overcoming the Huks, President Magsaysay was able to gather enough support from the Philippine legislature to pass land reform laws. These measures broke up some of the large tracts of land that wealthy Filipinos owned. The government redistributed much of this land to the tenant farm families who had worked the fields for decades.

Under Magsaysay's administration, foreign investment grew, and the economy improved. Magsaysay, known for his fairness and effectiveness, died in a plane crash in 1957. The administrations that followed attempted to break up even more of the huge tracts held by wealthy landowners. But landowners were politically powerful, and they blocked the reforms that these governments introduced.

Diosdado Macapagal, who became president in 1961, started another land reform program but met with limited success. Dissatisfaction with Macapagal's ineffective leadership grew. In the 1965 election Ferdinand Marcos, a member of the Philippine legislature, won the presidency.

The Marcos Era

During his first term as president, Marcos pushed forward two programs that won him loyalty from many Filipinos. One was a new strain of rice that yielded larger crops, providing more food for the country. The other was the completion of many public works projects. New buildings, roads, and bridges appeared throughout the islands. Marcos personally delivered paychecks to many of the datu (leaders)

Independent Picture Service

Ramón Magsaysay *(waving to the crowd)* served the Philippines as secretary of defense and was elected president in 1953. A popular politician throughout much of the country, Magsaysay helped bring order and prosperity to the nation.

Courtesy of Martin Luther King Library, Washington, D.C.

From northern Luzon, Ferdinand Marcos was a member of the national legislature before becoming president of the Philippines in 1965.

A band of Moro (Muslim) soldiers patrols part of Mindanao. The Muslim rebels are dedicated to establishing their own nation separate from the Philippines. Another group, the New People's Army, is made up of Communists who seek to overthrow the Philippine government on Luzon and other islands.

and barangay (village) laborers who had worked on the projects.

Marcos won a second term in 1969, and his administration faced new difficulties. Economic progress slowed, and the standard of living for the average Filipino fell. Muslim groups on Mindanao grew increasingly resentful of the growing Christian population on the island. They organized the Moro National Liberation Front (MNLF). These Muslims armed themselves and sought self-rule in the southern islands.

Another problem for Marcos and his government was a reborn Communist presence, called the New People's Army (NPA). Members of this group wanted more land reform and a political revolution. These rebels had especially strong support on the main island of Luzon.

During these years, Marcos supported the U.S. role in the Vietnam War. The U.S. military bases at Subic Bay and Clark Air Base on Luzon were important to the U.S. effort in Vietnam. Many Filipinos recognized the U.S. military presence as a continuation of the colonial bond between the two countries. Filipino nationalists rearded the United States with hostility.

Filipino students demonstrated in 1971 against the presence of the U.S. bases in the Philippines. Rally leaders also spoke against Marcos's failure to achieve economic reforms. As they tried to break up a demonstration in May 1972, national police killed dozens and wounded hundreds of protesters. In September 1972, a group of assassins unsuccessfully tried to kill the secretary of national defense, Juan

Photo by Ken Meter

Many Filipino landowners have set up lookout posts with armed guards to protect their crops from Communist guerrilla fighters.

Ponce Enrile. These violent events contributed to an atmosphere of unrest within the country.

Martial Law

In response to increasing difficulties, Marcos declared martial law (rule by the military) in 1972. Marcos took away the right of Filipinos to meet for political purposes, dissolved the constitution and the congress, and controlled the news media. He also limited the civil rights of Filipino citizens and arrested many of his opponents. Marcos exercised absolute power and only rarely sought public support through referendums (nationwide votes) on specific programs.

In 1973 a new constitution gave Marcos free rein to rule the country and an unlimited term of office. Marcos shared his power with a small group of supporters—including his wife, Imelda. During the 1970s, many Filipinos began to recognize that the Marcos administration was unable to solve the economic and political problems of the country. Others suspected Marcos of taking huge amounts of money for himself from the foreign loans made to the nation. (In 1988 the United States charged Marcos with stealing many millions of dollars that it had loaned to the Philippines for economic development.)

Under increasing pressure from the Filipino Roman Catholic Church to reestablish democratic elections and to observe human rights, Marcos ended martial law in 1981. Marcos won the presidency again that year in an election that observers said was dishonest. Many Filipinos began calling for a change of national leadership.

Benigno and Corazon Aquino

One of Marcos's opponents who had been arrested under martial law was Benigno Aquino. In 1977 a court established by Marcos had falsely convicted Aquino of murder and possession of firearms and had sentenced him to death. Filipinos believed that the conviction was politically motivated, and public pressure forced Marcos to lift the execution order. In 1980 the government released Aquino, giving him permission to travel to the United States for medical treatment. The opposition leader remained in exile for three years.

In 1983 Aquino was determined to return to the Philippines to lead a movement

Photo by UPI/Bettmann Newsphotos

In 1980 Benigno Aquino appeared at a press conference before he traveled to the United States for medical treatment. Aquino pressured the Marcos government to lift martial law (rule by the military) and to increase democratic participation.

for democratic reform. Although his closest advisers—including his wife, Corazon —discouraged his return to the Philippines, Aquino left the United States in August 1983. Soon after exiting the airplane at Manila airport, he was assassinated. Courts that Marcos controlled charged members of the armed forces with the crime, but the accused were found not guilty after a nine-month trial.

The court's finding did not convince most Filipinos and members of foreign governments of the army's innocence. Observers believed that Marcos was responsible for Aquino's assassination. Marcos felt pressure to restore confidence in his administration and to reopen the democratic channels of government. In November 1985, Marcos called for a presidential election to be held in February 1986.

ELECTIONS OF 1986

Marcos wanted to hold the election quickly because the politicians opposing him were still disorganized after Benigno Aquino's death. Although she had little political experience, Corazon Aquino became the main candidate opposing Marcos. A national commission with strong ties to Marcos counted the votes in the 1986 election, but several international observers also kept track of the tally. When the government commission proclaimed Marcos the winner, these observers accused him and the commission of falsifying the election results.

Photo by UPI/Bettmann Newsphotos

Benigno Aquino was assassinated at Manila Airport when he returned to the Philippines in 1983. Another man's corpse (background) **was said to be that of Aquino's killer, but investigators think the second body may have been put there to draw attention away from the real assassins.**

Photo by Ken Meter

Filipinos lined up to vote for their candidate in the presidential elections of 1986. Marcos was declared the winner, but international observers accused him of election fraud.

Photo by Ken Meter

In 1986 political rallies and marches occurred frequently in Manila and other Filipino cities, and sometimes the participants ended up in confrontations with police.

Ferdinand and Imelda Marcos left the Philippines in March 1986. Many foreign governments believed the charges of voter fraud and corruption that were leveled at the Marcos administration. Without substantial support from inside or outside the country, the Marcoses went into exile. The former president and his wife have been accused of stealing huge amounts of money from the Philippine government. They are on trial in the United States for taking U.S. foreign aid that was destined for economic development projects in the Philippines.

Photo by Reuters/Bettmann Newsphotos

Marcos received little support from the leaders of other nations, who pressured him to step aside in favor of Corazon Aquino. Members of the military who supported Aquino set up a rebel headquarters in a police building in Manila. When Marcos's troops threatened the rebels with tanks, huge crowds of Filipinos surrounded the police building, protecting the rebels from Marcos's soldiers.

Without popular or international support, Marcos and his family fled to Hawaii in early March 1986. Marcos's exit ended his 21-year rule of the Philippines. Corazon Aquino took office on February 25, 1986.

The Late 1980s

After becoming president of the Philippines, Corazon Aquino quickly restored freedom of the press and the full rights of citizens. The new chief executive also replaced corrupt government officials and suspended Marcos's 1973 constitution. In February 1987, 76 percent of eligible voters approved a new constitution. According to this national charter, Aquino would hold office until 1992.

Photo by Ken Meter

Many soldiers rejoiced after Corazon Aquino became president of the country. Military support of Benigno Aquino's widow helped her to establish her authority.

Aquino tried to make peace with the New People's Army, which had 30,000 soldiers by the late 1980s. After several unsuccessful attempts to negotiate a cease-fire, the Aquino government decided to attack the guerrillas directly. Similarly, in negotiations with the MNLF, Aquino offered partial self-rule to four largely Muslim provinces on the island of Mindanao. But when the Muslims broke a truce agreement in early 1988, fighting resumed between government troops and MNLF soldiers.

The slow pace of economic reform under Aquino dissatisfied many Filipinos. In 1989 inflation remained high, and wages continued to be low for most Filipino workers. Besides economic difficulties, Aquino has dealt with attempts by some military officers to overthrow her administration. The president, however, despite internal rivalry, continues to work for economic and political progress in the Philippines.

Government

The Constitution of 1987 provides for a bicameral (two-house) legislature. The senate contains 24 members, who are elected on a nationwide basis to six-year terms. Senators must be at least 35 years of age and may serve no more than two consecutive terms. The house of representatives has 200 members elected by districts for terms of three years. The president may appoint up to 50 additional representatives from among the nation's minority groups. Representatives must be at least 25 years old and can serve only three terms in a row.

The president directs the executive branch of government and is limited to one six-year term. Presidents must be at least 40 years old when elected. The chief executive signs bills passed by the legislature and also acts as commander in chief. The president names the cabinet members, but they must be approved by the legislature's Commission of Appointments.

Photo by Ken Meter

Corazon Aquino began her presidency on a great wave of popularity. Her administration has tackled the difficult problems of land reform and sluggish economic growth. Her government has begun to make progress slowly.

The Philippines's highest judicial body is the supreme court, which consists of a chief justice and 14 associate justices. The president appoints these justices to terms of four years. The court of appeals has a presiding judge and 35 associate justices. Local courts exist in every city.

The republic is divided into 13 regions, which are further broken down into a total of 73 provinces. Councils guide the regions, and a governor and two provincial board members rule each province. All officials at the local level are elected by their communities.

Courtesy of Philippine Department of Tourism, Manila

Fort Santiago in the Intramuros section of Manila is a popular gathering place for Filipinos as well as for tourists. Built by the Spanish, this old section of the city reflects its colonial past. The nearby museum dedicated to José Rizal commemorates the national independence movement.

3) The People

More than 65 million people live in the Philippines, and the majority are descended from Malay ancestors. Waves of Malay immigrants settled in various regions of the country and over time developed into many distinct ethnic groups. In addition to the Malay immigrants, Aeta, Chinese, Arab, and Spanish people also made their way to the archipelago. Offspring from marriages between Chinese or Spanish people and Malays became known as mestizos. The name *Filipinos*—at first used to

An Ifugao man stands on a terrace wall that also serves as a pathway through rice fields on the mountainside. Many members of the Ifugao ethnic group live in the highlands of northern Luzon.

describe people born of Spanish parents on the islands—is now a general name for all citizens of the country.

Ethnic Groups

The Philippines contains over 80 different ethnic groups. Many of these peoples, such as the descendants of the Aeta, live in remote parts of the islands. Their small communities have little contact with other villages. The Tagalog name for the many mountain-dwelling ethnic groups is Igorot, which means "mountaineer." The Bontoc and Ifugao are Malay-descended Igorots whose ancestors built the rice terraces on the mountainsides of northern Luzon.

The Tagalogs are a lowland people who live on southern Luzon and on Mindoro. The most numerous of the ethnic groups

These children belong to the Tagalog ethnic group, many of whose members live in southern Luzon and near Manila, where rice is the principal crop.

41

on the islands, the Tagalogs make up almost 25 percent of the Filipino population. Because their regional home includes Manila, many Tagalogs play a highly visible role in Filipino politics and business.

The Ilocanos form another ethnic group of Malay ancestry, and for the most part they reside on the western coast of Luzon and in the Cagayan Valley. The Ilocanos have moved into prominence in Philippine life in part because Ferdinand Marcos—a member of the Ilocano—gave many of them government jobs during his presidency. The Pampangans, on the other hand, have been largely excluded from the national mainstream. Living mostly in the central plain, many Pampangans are members of the Huk movement and other revolutionary parties.

The ethnic groups of the Visayan Islands also use the name Visayan to describe their entire population. The Cebuano, Waray-Waray, and Ilongo are three of the ethnic subgroups that make up the Visayan people. Many of the groups in this region grow and process sugarcane.

To make brightly colored cloth, an Igorot weaver still uses the dyes and patterns that her ancestors created centuries ago.

Igorot villagers use stones, palms, and timber to construct their homes in the mountains of Luzon.

42

Muslims in the southern islands, especially Mindanao, follow the Islamic command to pray five times daily while facing in the direction of Mecca—Islam's holy city in Saudi Arabia.

Courtesy of Philippine Department of Tourism, Manila

Independent Picture Service

Colorfully decorated sails are trademarks of Moro boats. These Muslims fish the waters of Mindanao and the Sulu Archipelago.

Filipino Muslims, who inhabit Mindanao and the Sulu Archipelago, include the Maranao, Samal, and Yakan ethnic groups. In general, the Muslims form a religious minority in the Philippines, but they are the dominant faith in the areas that they occupy. The legal system, religious language (Arabic), and culture of the Muslims set them apart from the rest of the nation.

Religion

Nearly 85 percent of the population of the Philippines is Roman Catholic. Spanish missionaries brought the religion to the islands in the sixteenth century. For several hundred years, membership in the clergy was restricted to Spaniards. In the late 1980s, however, most of the Catholic priests in the Philippines had been born there.

43

Each year, Roman Catholic Filipinos visit the graves of their dead family members on All Souls' Day. The faithful bring food, flowers, and candles to a celebration that includes prayers, singing, and remembrance.

This Roman Catholic church at Miagao on Panay Island is an example of Spanish-style architecture from the eighteenth century. Builders have added a distinctly Filipino touch by carving images of native plants into the facade of the building.

Small neighborhood houses of worship in poor communities are often made from wood, cinder block, and fiberglass sheeting.

Courtesy of Jodi M. Bantley

At the turn of the twentieth century, Gregorio Aglipay began the Independent Philippine Church as an offshoot of the Roman Catholic Church. In the late 1980s, this church's membership was about 5 percent of the Filipino population. A distinctive feature of Aglipay's church is its focus on Philippine patriotism, but this religious body also follows many Catholic doctrines. Other nationalistic Christian churches have grown up in recent decades, including the small but highly organized Iglesia ni Kristo.

Many Protestant sects developed roots in the Philippines beginning in the early 1900s. Small congregations of Episcopalians, Baptists, Lutherans, Methodists, and Presbyterians exist on the nation's principal islands. The Protestant groups have built and staffed many clinics and schools throughout the country.

Most followers of Islam—Muslims who are often called Moros—live on Mindanao Island and in the Sulu Archipelago. The practices of Islam include praying five times each day, fasting during the holy month of Ramadan, donating to the poor, and, if possible, traveling at least once to Mecca—the central city of Islam in Saudi

Courtesy of Philippine Department of Tourism, Manila

The clothes of this Muslim man reveal the traditional styles that are still popular among members of the Bukidnon people on Mindanao.

45

Arabia. The Koran—which records the visions received by Muhammad, the religion's founder—is the Islamic holy book. Muslims in the Philippines often feel greater bonds with Muslims in Malaysia and in the rest of the Islamic world than they do with the Christian population in their own country.

Languages and Education

More than 80 languages and dialects are spoken throughout the Philippines. Most of them are part of the Malayo-Polynesian family of languages. Tagalog is used on western Luzon, and Ilocano is the main tongue on the northern part of the island. Cebuano is the chief language spoken by the ethnic groups on the Visayan Islands.

In an effort to establish a deeper sense of national unity, the government designated Pilipino as the country's official language. Based on Tagalog, Pilipino has been accepted by over 50 percent of the population and is part of the course of studies in all the nation's schools.

Almost half of the population—including most businesspeople, lawyers, government workers, doctors, and educators—speak English. Spanish, which was widely spoken in the eighteenth and nineteenth centuries, is becoming rare.

About 83 percent of Filipinos can read and write. This literacy rate reflects the emphasis that Filipinos put on education. Public schools provide six years of free elementary education to all Filipino children. In the first two years of a child's schooling, instructors use the language of the region. After the second year, Pilipino and English become the main teaching languages.

Students begin secondary school at age 13 and continue for four years. Taught mainly in English, students focus on general studies in the first two years and on either college preparatory or vocational courses in the second two years. The government pays for secondary schooling in some areas of the country. Sixty percent of Filipinos who are aged 13 to 17 attend secondary classes.

Filipino children line up in a schoolyard before they begin their day of classes. Elementary education is free in the Philippines, and all school-age children are required to attend.

A Filipino teacher guides her students in reading their Pilipino textbooks. Pupils take courses both in their national language, Pilipino, and in English.

The Philippines has many colleges and universities, located primarily in Manila. Students from all parts of Southeast Asia come to the islands to complete their education. The University of the East, Santo Tomás University, Feati University, and the University of the Philippines are all within metropolitan Manila. These institutions offer a wide range of liberal arts and professional courses. Bicol University at Legazpi and Saint Louis University at Baguio are two of the postsecondary schools located outside of Manila.

Health

The physical health of Filipinos has improved significantly since the mid-1970s. With dietary information and food supplements, the government attacked the

In 1611 Roman Catholic missionaries in Manila founded Santo Tomás University—one of the oldest institutions of higher learning in Asia. During World War II, the Japanese used the campus as a concentration camp for U.S. prisoners of war.

47

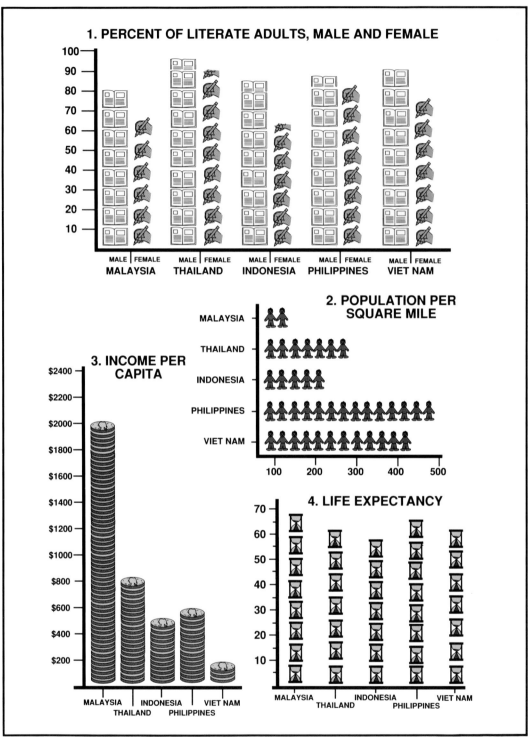

1. PERCENT OF LITERATE ADULTS, MALE AND FEMALE

2. POPULATION PER SQUARE MILE

3. INCOME PER CAPITA

4. LIFE EXPECTANCY

Artwork by Mindy A. Rabin

Depicted in this chart are factors relating to the standard of living in five countries in southeastern Asia. Information taken from "1987 World Population Data Sheet," "The World's Women: A Profile," and "Children of the World" compiled by the Population Reference Bureau, Washington, D.C.

48

Mothers and children gather at a nutrition center sponsored by the government and by religious organizations. At these centers, the children receive food supplements, and the mothers learn about health care.

On Negros, an island in the central Philippines, workers make nutritious cookies out of a mixture of soy flour and peanuts. The food is distributed to youngsters throughout the region.

population's poor nutritional practices. As a result, the health of mothers and their infants has been enhanced, and life expectancy figures have risen. In 1989 about 48 babies among every 1,000 newborns died within their first year of life. Although somewhat high, this figure compares favorably with the average rate of 68 per 1,000 in all of Southeast Asia. The Philippine life expectancy of 66 years also was better than the regional average of 61.

The Philippine government is striving to distribute health-care workers throughout the country. Of the 15,000 doctors on the islands in the late 1980s, one-third practiced medicine in Manila. Of the 1,600 hospitals in the nation, one-fourth were located in the capital city.

In an effort to provide basic health care to the country's rural population, the government has trained paramedics in disease control, sanitation, and nutrition. These new medical professionals are stationed in rural areas. Among the principal illnesses that Filipino medical workers treat are malaria, pneumonia, intestinal diseases, and bronchitis.

One cause of concern to those in charge of national health policies is the country's high population growth rate. In 1989 the population increased by 2.8 percent. At that rate, the number of Filipinos will double in 25 years. Religious beliefs that prohibit birth control and the Philippine tradition of large families make population increases difficult to hold in check. High rates of population growth strain food resources, cause overcrowding in urban areas, and mean that a higher percentage of Filipinos will be likely to live in poverty.

Many Filipino ethnic groups weave intricately designed cloth in bold hues. Skilled artisans take many hours to finish a piece of woven fabric on a handloom.

On the island of Mindanao, a woman performs a dance that has been handed on for generations in her ethnic community.

The Arts

Filipinos have expressed themselves for centuries in the arts of music, dance, painting, and literature. The culture of the Philippines is a mixture of Malay, Chinese, Spanish, Arab, and U.S. influences. These styles influence both the folk traditions and fine arts of the nation.

Filipinos perform Western classical music and compose their own contemporary works. Many Filipinos write rock songs in Pilipino or English and often perform their music in other Southeast Asian countries. Ethnic music is popular at village festivals, and the musicians use bamboo flutes, gongs, bamboo guitars, and *git-gits* (fiddles).

Filipino ethnic dances often draw their themes from the world of nature. On Leyte Island, dancers often perform the *tinikling*, which represents the flight of the heron. The National Ballet Federation sponsors Filipinos as they study and perform classical Western ballet. Modern dance also holds a prominent place in the nation's cultural life.

Many visual artists have worked in the Philippines since the early 1800s, when Spanish influence was especially strong. The painter Felix Resureccion Hidalgo is the most famous Filipino artist of the colonial period. Juan Luna, another colonial-era painter, employed a realistic style and also gained international fame.

Sculptor Guillermo Tolentino, who became the official artist of the nation in 1973, is famous for his classical artworks. Since the early twentieth century, many filmmakers have also worked in the Philippines, producing popular movies in English and Pilipino.

At the close of the nineteenth century, José Rizal, the Philippine independence leader, wrote a novel that has become a national classic, *Noli Me Tangere* (Touch Me Not). Written in Spanish, Rizal's powerful stories focus on the Filipino search for self-rule. Modern-day Filipino novelists and poets write in Pilipino and English.

Sports and Recreation

Traditional sports in the Philippines include *arnis*—a form of sword combat that uses wooden sticks—and *sipa*, which resembles volleyball. Filipinos also enjoy playing basketball and compete on organized teams in schools and at the professional level. Baseball and jai alai—a high-speed game played on a long, open-air court—are also major national sports.

Chess is another popular pastime. Played by Filipinos of many ages, chess matches occur in both urban and rural areas. The Philippines has supplied several grandmasters to the international chess tour.

Tupada (gamecock fights) occur in most of the villages, towns, and cities of the country. Competitors put their roosters—which are fitted with sharp blades behind one leg—into a pit to do battle until one of the animals wounds the other. A centuries-old spectator sport, tupada is a recreation that continues to entertain many Filipinos.

Food

Filipino food combines Malay, Chinese, Arab, and Spanish influences. Rice and seafood are the main ingredients in daily fare. Seafood from the nation's coastal waters is often cooked over coals or prepared raw in a sauce called *kilawin*. Filipino fish soup—*sinigang*—is often made from a base of tamarind (a tropical fruit) that has a tangy, sour taste.

Among the best-known Filipino dishes is *adobo,* a Spanish-style stew made from chicken and pork and cooked with vinegar and garlic. The dish's Chinese influence comes out in its use of soy sauce. Another distinctive Filipino food is *lechon* (roasted pork), which is served at festivals. During national holidays and at large family gatherings, a whole pig is roasted by turning it slowly over coals. Other typical Filipino foods include pasta noodles called *pancit,* and eggrolls called *lumpia,* which cooks make from pork and cabbage.

Courtesy of Philippine Department of Tourism, Manila

Young Filipino men compete for fruits and vegetables suspended in the air. Both food and games are important elements of Philippine fiestas.

Courtesy of Jodi M. Bantley

Streetside vendors sell their fish, one of the Philippines' main forms of protein. Such markets are found throughout the country's small towns and villages.

Filipinos use coconuts to make soups and to brew an alcoholic beverage called *lambanog.* Coconut milk—an ingredient that reflects Malay influence—is used to flavor meats and vegetables. Common Filipino fruits include mangoes, bananas, rambutans (red, oval-shaped fruit), watermelons, and papayas. Cooks of the islands often mix a number of fruits together into a delicious salad called *halo-halo.*

A food seller sits amid baskets of fresh produce in Baguio.

4) The Economy

In the late 1980s, the Philippines was recovering from the economic difficulties it experienced early in the decade. After several years of economic decline, the nation's gross domestic product, or GDP (the value of goods and services produced annually in the country), began to increase at an annual rate of about 5 percent. The economy recovered mostly because of rising prices for Philippine agricultural exports. The government also changed tax and credit policies in order to encourage foreign investment and to increase the number of loans to businesspeople and farmers.

Half of the Filipino work force is involved in agriculture, forestry, and fishing, and these workers produce 26 percent of the GDP. About 15 percent of the Filipino labor pool is employed in industrial plants. Another 35 percent fills service industries, which include government, education, trade, transportation, finance, and communication.

Agriculture

Farms in the Philippines range from small, rented plots to large, mechanized plantations. Most farming families own or rent fields that average seven acres. Attempts at land reform allowed more Filipinos to hold property, but much of the nation's land still belongs to a relatively small group of landowners.

Farmers cultivate 35 percent of the country, and of that area about two-thirds is used to raise rice and corn. Researchers are investigating ways to increase the production of these major food crops. The irrigated farms of central Luzon grow high-yield rice crops, as do the Cagayan Valley and the western Visayan Islands. Corn thrives in the upland areas of Mindanao and on many of the Visayan Islands.

Although rice and corn volumes increased in the 1980s, dry weather during the 1987 growing season made it necessary for the country to import these food items in 1988. Other food crops include sweet potatoes and cassavas (starchy root crops).

Filipino farmers cultivate some crops —including bananas, pineapples, mangoes,

Coconuts that have been split into halves dry in the sun along a highway. The meat of the coconut, which appears in many Filipino dishes, is one of the country's most important commercial crops.

Courtesy of Jodi M. Bantley

Courtesy of Agency for International Development

Rice farming in the Philippines requires a great deal of hand labor *(above)*. Seedlings are transplanted into flooded fields *(right)* when they are 30 to 40 days old. They grow rapidly in the hot climate.

and coconuts—both for local demand and for export. Coconuts, which are grown along the coastal areas, bring in nearly 10 percent of the nation's export earnings. Workers process coconuts into copra—dried coconut meat—or into oil. Sugarcane, another major export crop, thrives on western and northeastern Negros and on central Luzon. Abaca plants provide fiber from which workers make a strong rope known as Manila hemp. Plantations and small farms alike cultivate rubber and tobacco crops that are sold abroad.

Courtesy of Agency for International Development

Photo by Ken Meter

Small walls of earth hold water in the rice paddies.

Photo by Ken Meter

Since the early 1700s, Filipinos have grown and refined sugarcane—an important export crop.

Independent Picture Service

Coils of rope made from Manila hemp will be used to tie ships to piers.

Manufacturing

Most of the industries of the Philippines are located in or near Manila. Smaller factories process sugarcane, coconuts, tobacco, abaca, and latex from rubber trees.

Traditional farming techniques—for example, using a water buffalo and wooden plow—are still important in the Philippines, although mechanized methods are becoming more common.

Photo by Ken Meter

Other manufacturers produce textiles, paper products, electronics, furniture, and medicinal drugs. Filipinos also work in heavy industry, making cement, fertilizers, chemicals, steel, and glass. The manufacturing sector contributes 25 percent of the Philippine GDP.

After growing steadily since the 1950s, profits from manufacturing fell each year in the early 1980s. The output of factories increased in 1986, but labor strikes hampered the continued development of the industrial sector. In 1986 the government sold many of the companies that Marcos had nationalized (put under state ownership), returning over 100 businesses to the private sphere. Aquino's administration has also encouraged foreign and domestic investment by offering tax breaks and generous credit terms.

The Philippines continues to import more manufactured goods—especially heavy machinery—than it produces. Textiles and electronics are among the nation's major exports. The government has encouraged new industries to develop, especially on

Photo by Ken Meter

Textile production is the fourth largest manufacturing industry in the Philippines and employs many young Filipinos.

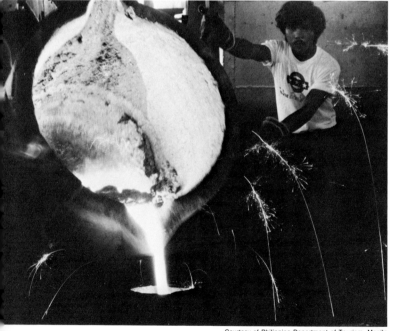

Courtesy of Philippine Department of Tourism, Manila

A factory worker pours melted steel, which is processed from iron ore. The Philippines also has rich deposits of copper, gold, chromite, coal, limestone, manganese, nickel, silver, and zinc.

This machine polishes a slab of marble, which was taken from quarries (excavation sites) in the Philippines.

Courtesy of Philippine Department of Tourism, Manila

Courtesy of Philippine Department of Tourism, Manila

Using cages *(above)* to hold pearl-producing oysters, the people of the southern Philippines cultivate these shellfish in coastal farms. The Gloria Maris—one of the world's largest and most famous pearls—came from Philippine waters.

sites away from Manila. These new manufacturing plants may help to raise new money for the country's treasury.

Fishing

With many miles of coastline and with most of its population living near the sea, the Philippines has long been a fishing nation. Filipinos eat freshly caught fish at many of their meals. They are developing refrigeration and processing plants that will enable them to store and transport fish products safely.

The islands lie within an ocean area that is rich in both its variety and quantity of seafood. Bonitos, shrimp, crabs, tuna, mackerel, anchovies, sardines, and swordfish are some of the species taken from Philippine waters. In the Sulu Archipelago, fishermen find large numbers of mollusks, which yield mother-of-pearl (a hard, pearly material) from the inner layer of their shells. This substance is often used in Filipino jewelry. Milkfish, tilapia, and shrimp grow in ponds that Filipinos have set up at the mouths of rivers and along the coasts.

57

A fisherman freshens his catch with seawater during the long trip from fishing grounds to market. One of the Philippines' most important products, seafood makes up a substantial part of the Filipino diet.

Courtesy of Philippine Department of Tourism, Manila

Small Camiguin Island, like much of the Philippines, is heavily forested. The country exports mahogany and many other kinds of timber.

Motorized trawlers, which drag huge nets behind them, make up over half of the commercial fishing fleet in the Philippines. Many Filipino fishermen, however, still use the traditional *bancas*—wooden-hulled fishing boats with outriggers (frames) that project from the side for stability. Crews on these boats cast lines or throw single nets by hand.

The government has attempted to regulate the number of boats working in over-fished areas—especially in Manila Bay —because further depletion of the fish stock could greatly reduce catches in the future. The Aquino administration also has encouraged Filipinos to develop deep-water fishing instead of relying on the nation's traditional coastal fishing grounds.

Courtesy of Jodi M. Bantley

Residents of fishing villages catch anchovies, mackerel, sardines, scad, tuna, and other species in the seas surrounding the Philippine Islands.

Loggers cut wood at a research center in a national forest. Funded by the Philippine government and the United Nations, the installation is part of a program that conducts research on tree species. The scheme also seeks to improve timber management and soil conservation methods.

Forestry and Mining

Forests cover almost half of the Philippines. More than 3,000 varieties of trees grow on the islands, but most of the lumber that is cut down for export is Philippine mahogany. Mangrove trees from the coastal areas are also an important commercial timber. Pine forests that thrive at high elevations, especially on Luzon and Mindoro, provide another lumber source. Ceiba trees yield kapok, a fiber that is used as stuffing in some mattresses and life preservers. Bamboo plants grow in groves throughout the islands. Construction workers use bamboo to build homes in rural areas, and craftspeople use it to make mats, baskets, and other items.

Uncontrolled logging has destroyed large areas of Philippine rain-forest. Without trees to anchor the soil, erosion occurs and is especially serious during the height of the monsoon rains. Farmers who cut and burn vegetation to clear new fields for cultivation have also damaged the nation's timber resources. Conservation and reforestation efforts sponsored by the government

A resident of Mindanao earns a living weaving mats from bamboo. Income on Mindanao—which is the second biggest island in the Philippines—comes mainly from agriculture.

began in the 1970s but have proceeded slowly. In the late 1980s, timber for export was in short supply in some areas of the country.

Independent Picture Service

A Filipino worker rakes crystallized salt from a salt bed. After seawater floods the beds, the liquid gradually evaporates, leaving behind large amounts of salt crystals.

The Philippines has large reserves of several minerals. Its copper, nickel, and chromite supplies are among the largest in the world. Miners have found gold on northern Luzon and in the mountains of Mindanao. Coal, iron ore, limestone, zinc, and silver are also mined in the islands. Declining prices for many of these minerals during the 1980s have reduced the amount of money available to search for additional deposits.

Transportation and Energy

The Philippines has one of the most developed transportation systems in Asia. Although the terrain of the islands is mountainous, the nation has more than 80,000 miles of roads, of which 65 percent are paved. Because few Filipinos own cars, jeepneys—brightly painted taxis—serve local transportation needs. The Philippine National Railway has over 1,100 miles of train track, most of which is on Luzon. A rapid transit system knits metropolitan Manila together by rail.

Large copper reserves exist in the Philippines. This mine is located in Marinduque, a small, circular island lying between Luzon and Mindoro.

Courtesy of Philippine Department of Tourism, Manila

61

Filipinos created jeepneys from U.S. Army surplus jeeps after World War II when transport was scarce on the island. The colorful vehicles are the most common form of land transportation in the Philippines, and more than 30,000 of them crisscross the streets of Manila.

Boat and airplane routes link the many islands of the Philippines. Manila, Cebu, and Davao are among the major inter-island ports for freighters that carry goods and for ferryboats that transport people. Small aircraft connect the islands, with Philippine Airlines serving as the nation's principal domestic and international carrier. Manila Airport is a hub for air traffic from all over the world.

To fuel vehicles and to provide energy for domestic and industrial use, the Philippines imports large quantities of petroleum. In 1986 oil purchases accounted for 16 percent of the total amount of imports. To encourage citizens to use other energy sources, the government put a 15 percent tax on oil products, making them more expensive for consumers to buy. Oil engineers have discovered petroleum off the coast of Palawan, but production in the 1980s supplied only 3 percent of the nation's energy needs.

Hydroelectricity and geothermal power (heat from within the earth) are two of the nation's most promising energy sources. In the late 1980s, plants along the nation's rivers provided about one-third of the country's power. Plans to establish small

Pipelines carry oil through the lush rain-forests of the Philippines. The nation is dependent on imported oil for most of its energy needs.

hydropower plants in rural areas were moving ahead slowly in 1989. The government built three geothermal sites in the mid-1980s and planned to construct several more. The Philippines is second only to the United States in its use of geothermal power.

The Future

Since Corazon Aquino's leadership began in 1986, the nation's economy grew slightly after years of debt and low productivity. More Filipinos were employed than during the closing years of the Marcos administration. Furthermore, the political rights that Marcos limited were restored. One of the challenges facing the Aquino administration is to continue these positive trends.

Not all groups are satisfied, however. In 1986 the Communist New People's Army rejected the government's offers of amnesty (pardon for crimes or political offenses) and employment training in return for laying down their weapons. In 1988 the Muslims of the Moro National Liberation Front demanded greater independence in southern Mindanao.

Despite the continued pressure of economic and political problems, the nation faces an even greater challenge—unchecked population growth. In early 1989, the government had not yet established plans to reduce the rising birthrate. Filipino observers think that countrywide action is needed to limit population growth. Until such action is taken, overcrowding, food shortages, and lack of jobs will probably continue to threaten the nation's progress.

Courtesy of UNICEF

Young Filipinos play in the coastal waters of one of the nation's many islands. Through education, the Philippines hopes to provide its children with the knowledge and skills that are needed to help the country grow stronger economically, politically, and socially.

Index